Charlie,
R.J. is from Erie
And sits Next to me
At American Legion
Meetings

Tom Young
803-648-2672
Tomyoung@allstate.com

The Invisible Veteran

Photography and Poetry of the Street

RJ Bednez

The Invisible Veteran

Photography and Poetry of the Streets

By RJ Bednez
Poet, Photographer, and Vietnam Veteran

Photo Expressions by BedNez
2018

Dedication

You can take the soldier out of combat but you cannot take combat out of the soldier.

I am dedicating this book to the forgotten veterans; who, without reservation, accepted the responsibility of defending our constitution against all enemies at home and abroad. We as a country speak highly of the men and women in uniform; we call them heroes and thank them for their service, when the uniform comes off the real challenge begins.

Upon discharge from the service, the veteran has to reenter society, they are expected to return to a normal life, when their life is anything but normal. Some veterans adjust with ease, some find it difficult and need assistance through counseling, others commit suicide, and there are those who try to adjust by using drugs, alcohol, or both, and many veterans end up living on the streets.

We see them every day, sleeping on park benches, gathering on street corners, going into or coming from soup kitchens. We see them every day but refuse to make eye contact. We cross the street to avoid them, they are just another lazy person refusing to work, looking for a handout; a burden on society.

I was raised to not judge a person until I have walked a mile in their shoes, these veterans have sacrificed their youth to serve us. The next time you see a person who is homeless, I hope you will take the time to hear his or her story and make an effort to understand their life.

Table of Contents

VI
Nate

VII
Tony

I
John

John is the inspiration of this book. I met John in Warren, PA. He is a Korean War Veteran, who lives in the Allegheny Forest during the summer months, and in Mexico, where his wife is buried, in the winter.

The Apology

It is with regret that I have forgotten my past,
I am guilty.
Consumed by my own trials and tribulations, I have walked past you unseen.
Hiding my feelings of failure and despair,
I have ignored your pain,
Even though it exists within me,
Maybe it's the fear that someday I may return,
Or maybe you remind me of the hell that exists in my dreams.

Today, I embrace my past,
It has made me who I am.
It has molded me and given me strength.
I see you my brother.
I understand your pain.
We are united in a common bond,
To me, you will never again be invisible.

II
Michael

Feel Me

How can you judge me?

You don't know me.

You cannot feel my pain,

My pain is invisible.

You have not traveled to where I have been.

My boots are old and stained with the blood of my brothers, sisters, and enemies.

You dare not walk in them.

How can you help me when you cannot feel my pain?

Lost Innocence

My body is tired and I must sleep.

This bench is where I lay my head.

My face covered to hide my identity,

Dreaming of better days.

I was young and innocent

Playing games of war,

My innocence is no more.

His Eyes

His eyes tell a story of pain and distrust.
His thoughts engrossed in times lost.

Each day is a challenge…
There is nowhere to go.

Pulling up the collar on his torn coat,
Into the frigid air he walks in worn out shoes.
His pockets… empty.

He reaches out his cold bare hand
Not to seek a handout.
His fellow man he helps.

<u>Voices</u>

The voices in my head will not be silenced.

They speak to me night and day.

The streets are my salvation.

I have no place to turn.

There is hatred in your eyes and repulsion in your voice.

You thank me for my service,

Then turn your back to me.

The voices tell me to beware.

III
Bob

Shattered Dreams

Shattered dreams
Like pieces of glass
To the ground they fall.

Roads to be traveled,
There is nowhere to go.

People all around me,
Loneliness took hold.

Light shining brightly…
Darkness, despair

Bound by the chains of depression,
There is struggling to be free.

Happiness eludes
To dreams that are shattered.

Reminders of War

Memories of past wars…

Ignorance of future wars….

Sitting in your castle of stone and marble,

You send us off to fight your battles,

Not knowing our names or from where we come.

As you feast upon the safety we provide,

You drink wine, as we drink blood.

You call us heroes by the light of day

And by night deprive us of what is ours.

When we no longer serve your purpose you toss us aside,

We are a creation of your self-serving arrogance.

Dreams

You invade my thoughts while sleeping.
It seems so real.

My mind begins to wander.
Sun begins to rise.
Eyes wide open,
You invade my thoughts.

I was killed in that forsaken land.
I just have not died.

Returning home,
You ignored my accomplishments.
You continue to invade my thoughts.

Sleepless nights,
Days filled with pain,
Emotionless,
You invade my dreams.

IV
Kevin

VISION

Even as a child I never felt that I belonged.

I feared the secrets that I concealed...

Loneliness and despair.

In complete darkness I walk when others have light.

Nowhere to turn

My voice cannot be heard.

I am unseen and silent.

I have ascended from the pit of hell.

I now walk with my head held high.

I have chosen to face my fears, and ignore the voices of condemnation.

I am free, I have seen the light.

Speaking Out

You look at me with repulsion.

Not knowing who I am.

You see only what you believe.

Your perception is your truth.

Without knowing you,

I protected your freedom.

Sacrifices I have made.

The memories that haunt me

Follow me to my grave.

I ask not for your pity.

I ask for respect.

Tossed Aside

Like broken toys in the attic

And dust on the floor.

Past dreams are forgotten.

Good times tossed aside.

Broken bodies in cardboard boxes

Dream of days past.

A time of innocence is changed by war.

A feeling of loneness and despair,

The stench of combat forever haunts me.

Words

You will never amount to anything.
These words are spoken daily.

You laugh at my mistakes.
Your superior presence
Still looks down on me.

I can overcome the physical abuse.
Pain subsides,
Your words cut deep.
Silent pain remains.

For years, I hated myself
More than I hated you.
Days are a struggle when you don't belong.
Nowhere to turn,
No place to run.

In private the tears do flow,
The feelings of emptiness,
No place to go.

You will not win.
This I guarantee.
Your words belittling,
From these chains I will break free.

Faith

You wear your religion like armor

Protecting you from what you care not to understand.

The Christian Bible your weapon

Steadfast holds in your hand.

Condemnation is your battle cry,

In the name of God, you belittle and crucify.

He walked among beggars, prostitutes, and thieves

With open arms, accepting them as his equal

Preaching love, acceptance, and forgiveness,

Promising a better life.

Are you more righteous than Jesus?

Or, do you just use his name to justify your fears?

Anger

Anger does not consume me

I have accepted where I am.

I served to protect your freedom.

Freedom of religion, choice, and sexual preference,

That is the strength of our nation and all that we stand for.

Our leaders today preach hatred not acceptance.

They seek to blame others for their injustice.

They divide us so that we become weak.

Encourage violence toward those who do not agree.

We are not a nation of brotherly love.

We are a nation of ignorance, bigotry, and anger.

V
Robert

Nightmares

Sleep does not come easy.

My mind wanders through the night's darkness.

Silence is my enemy.

Decades have passed, so many changes, and there are none.

The names, the sounds, and the smells remain with me.

Was it only yesterday?

You remove the warrior from combat.

Combat remains with the warrior.

Innocence Lost

You take our sons and daughters,
Gone is innocence and youth.

Put them in the uniform of our country's pride.
Teach them how to fight.
Hopefully survive.

Boots on the ground
Blood stained earth,
Armies marching forward,
Fear in their eyes.

Every day in combat,
A part of them dies.

The innocence they have lost
Never to return.

The hell they have witnessed,
Forever inside them burns.

Who Am I

I am your old friend…

I am your brother,

Your sister,

I am your father,

Your son,

I am your mother,

Your daughter,

I am a homeless veteran, and I am invisible.

<u>Choices</u>

The lines on my face,

A roadmap of my past,

Dull eyes looking downward

Dreading what the future may bring.

Have I hit bottom or do I have further to fall?

I look upward the sun hurts my eyes.

The rungs are loose and rotten.

I climb from the depths of hell.

The ladder supports my weight,

Toward the future I climb.

My eyes are adjusting to the bright light ahead.

It is easy to focus on my destination.

I have chosen to win.

VI

Nate

Combat

You cannot experience the hell of combat on your TV screen.

The comfort of a theater,

There is the uncertainty of your existence…

The tightness in your stomach,

The smells in the air,

The chaos,

The screams of suffering brothers…

These are the reality of combat and they remain with you forever.

Depression

My hands are numb.
The cold air cuts deep.
I haven't slept in days.

Looking for somewhere to rest
To warm my soul
Someplace to escape this darkness
This emptiness inside

I am surrounded by love.
I am alone.
I feel nothing…
Desperate

Accomplishments I have many.
Accomplishments I have none.

I fight these feelings of nonexistence
In darkness when there is light.

I know these feelings will soon pass
I cannot let go.

My hands are numb.
The cold air cuts deep.
I'm looking for a place to warm my soul.

The Stare

Alone with my thoughts I stare into the future.

Felling empty, alone, and depressed

How did I get here?

Perceived as a burden on society looking for a handout

I am a good person who served our country so that you can be free.

Freedom does not behold me.

Battling demons, loneliness, hunger, and my thoughts

I am embarrassed.

I was once productive and now I am lost.

How can I help myself?

I can't be found.

Strength

Face not your adversity,

Know not your strength.

I have not been defeated.

I have gained knowledge.

I relish in my victories.

They did not come easy.

I am a soldier and I know how to survive.

VII
Tony

<u>Imprisoned</u>

Drugs and alcohol have consumed my soul.

I was once young and strong.

Today I am broken and weak

For I have aged beyond my years.

My dreams are fading fast,

Soon they will be lost.

This hell that I have created,

Darkness like clockwork takes over the light.

The candle of life has stopped burning,

I look up,

I see nothing.

Is there no hope?

Welcome Home

As a young man I answered your call to duty,

Like a knight on a white stallion.

I bled red, white, and blue.

I wore my uniform with pride.

Returned home a man beyond my years,

The uniform a disgrace,

There were no hero parades.

My country turned its back on me,

I hung my head in shame.

Lost in the anger that consumed me

Loneliness I felt.

Faded into the landscape

Like a forgotten toy.

Isolation became my paradise.

My past is a private hell.

<u>Denial</u>

I called out your name.

There was no answer.

You plugged your ears,

Silence...

You covered your eyes,

Darkness...

I exist no more.

Acknowledgement

If I were to acknowledge everyone who supported me in this adventure, I would have more pages in the acknowledgement than the books body.
That being said, I must recognize The Independence House in Erie Pennsylvania for providing shelter and counselling to veterans in need. I thank the veterans who gave me permission to photograph them and were willing to share their stories. Finally I thank my wife Pam, who has been my rock for over thirty three years.

In Memory

Sadly from the beginning of this project to its completion, Michael and Nate have lost their battles with the demons that possessed them. Rest in peace my brothers and thank you for your service. My heart is heavy with the news of your passing and my life is richer from knowing you.

90896537R00042

Made in the USA
Middletown, DE
26 September 2018